Remembering Mama

REMEMBERING MAMA

Large-quantity purchases or custom editions of this book are available at a discount from the publisher. For more information, contact the sales department at Augsburg Fortress, Publishers, 1-800-328-4648, or write to: Sales Director, Augsburg Fortress, Publishers, P.O. Box 1209, Minneapolis, MN 55440-1209.

Song text on pages 23 and 24 © Board of Publication, Lutheran Church in America, admin. Augsburg Fortress.

Cover and book design by Michelle L. N. Cook and Angela L. Chostner
Illustrations by Angela L. Chostner

Library of Congress Cataloging-in-Publication Data
Dokas, Dara, 1968-
   Remembering Mama / by Dara Dokas; illustrated by Angela L. Chostner.
      p. cm.
   Summary: A fictional story illustrates different emotional reactions to the loss of a parent, and a variety of nonfiction activities are suggested to help express grief.
   ISBN 0-8066-4352-8 (alk. paper)
      1. Grief in children—Juvenile literature. 2. Bereavement in children—Juvenile literature. 3. Mothers—Death—Psychological aspects—Juvenile literature. 4. Children and death—Juvenile literature. 5. Loss (Psychology) in children—Juvenile literature. [1. Grief. 2. Death. 3. Mothers. 4. Christian life.] I. Chostner, Angela L., 1964- ill. II. Title.
BF723.G75 D65 2002
155.9'37'083—dc21   2001053283

The paper used in this publication meets the minimum requirements of American National Standard for Information Sciences—Permanence of Paper for Printed Library Materials, ANSI Z329.48-1984. ♾ ™

Printed in China   AF 9-4352

06   05   04   03   02   1   2   3   4   5   6   7   8   9   10

Remembering Mama

✷ Written by Dara Dokas ✷
Illustrated by Angela L. Chostner

Augsburg Books
Bringing Families Together
for Children & Families

For Paul, with love and gratitude
   —D. D.

To those who lost loved ones
on September 11, 2001
   —A. L. C.

When I remember Mama . . .

I always think of flowers.
Mama loved flowers.
That's what everyone says.

Dad tells me about the day he met Mama,
how she had a bright white daisy in her
dark, dark hair.

Grandma talks about Mama's garden
with yellow daffodils, tiny blue bells,
and tulips, striped and feathery.

On days when I feel sad
that Mama died, and clouds
hang like a heavy, gray afghan
in the sky, Dad tells me how
much Mama loved me and how
she knew I loved her, too.

Dad says heaven is not far away.
Mama is still close by, and she is with God.

I think heaven must have a big garden
for Mama to enjoy. As I look up at the sky,
heaven seems closer on a cloudy day.

On days when I feel mad at
Mama for leaving me behind,
Dad and I sit near the Frazier
fir that Mama planted in the
backyard so the animals could
have a Christmas tree, too.

I breathe in the thick smell
of pine and think of Mama.

I remember how Mama
smelled, sometimes like lilac
and sometimes like rain.

People ask, "Is is hard to remember her?" Sometimes.

But, Dad and I talk about Mama. How she loved music and was always humming and tapping her foot to the beat.

How she told the same grasshopper joke over and over and laughed so hard that we laughed, too.

And how she said good night to all her ferns,
philodendrons, and the spotted prayer plant
that folds its leaves in prayer each night.
That helps me remember.

Grandma sometimes shows me pictures.
Mama riding her bicycle with me on the back.
Mama helping me pat down the earth over
new iris bulbs. That helps, too.

But some things I remember on my own.
Mama's hair tickling my face as she bent
down to tuck me in, her soft kisses on my
cheek goodnight, her voice, strong and low,
singing "Children of the Heavenly Father"
to me, as I fell asleep,

and her flowers. I remember
Mama singing to her flowers.

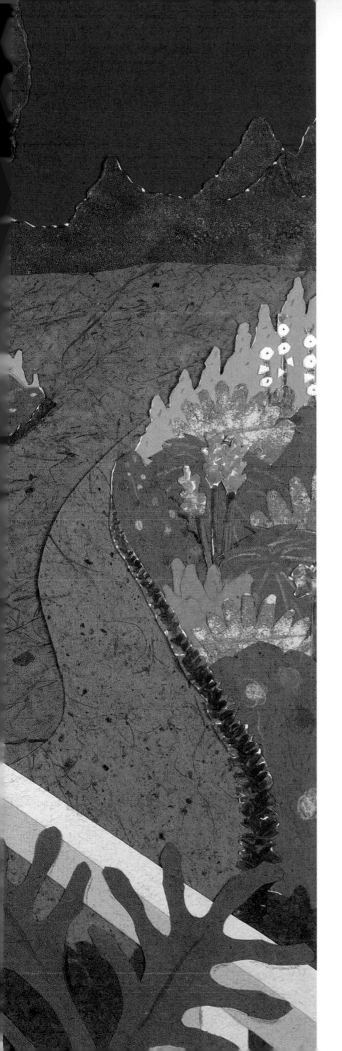

Now sometimes when Dad
sits in the rocking chair, not
rocking, just looking out at
Mama's garden,

I climb into the chair with him
and I start to sing Mama's song:
"Children of the heavenly
Father, safely in his bosom
gather . . ."

Dad joins in with his deep voice.
But we are both off key and we
begin to smile.

"Nestling bird or star in heaven,
such a refuge ne'er was given."

As we rock together and sing, I think of Mama,

nearby in heaven, tending God's flowers and singing along.

Thoughts for Kids

In *Remembering Mama,* the young girl sometimes feels very sad, while other times she feels mad that her mother has died. You may feel the same way, or you may have different feelings. Remember, however you are feeling, it is normal. Here are some things you can do when someone you love dies.

Talk to Someone

The most important thing you can do is talk to someone about what you are thinking and how you are feeling. You can talk to a parent, grandparent, another family member, pastor, youth leader, teacher, counselor, or a family friend.

Keep a Journal

A journal is a place to write down your private thoughts and feelings. You can use a notebook or a blank book. You can write poems, stories, and memories. You can draw pictures and add photos. Your journal is for you, but you can share it with someone else if you like.

Write Letters

Writing letters to the person who is gone is a good way to say what you would like to tell them. Even though the person is not here to read the letter, writing it can make you feel better. You can also write a letter to God if you want. It's okay to share your letters with someone or just keep them in a private place.

Start a Memory Box

A memory box is a special place to put letters, drawings, poems, lists of memories, and photos. You can also put things in your memory box that used to belong to the person who is gone or that remind you of him or her. Some items may be a piece of jewelry, a favorite book, a scarf, gloves, or even a favorite sweater. Sometimes, having something you can hold and smell and touch helps bring memories of the person back to you. If you like, ask other people to add something to your memory box.

Let It Out

If you are sad, you can cry. If you are mad, you can scream into your pillow or do something active. You can talk about it or write about it. Best of all, you can get a big hug from someone you love.

Look at Photos

Look through a photo album or your memory box with someone you love to remember the person who died. Talk about what you remember and how you feel. Some memories may make you cry and others may make you laugh. Both are okay.

Pray

Praying to God is a good way to let your feelings be heard. God loves you very much and cares about how you are feeling. It's okay to pray alone or with someone else.

Plant a Tree or Flowers

You can plant a special tree or flower garden in memory of the person who has died. As the tree grows and the flowers bloom, you will be reminded of the person you love.

Be Physical

Doing something physical will help you feel better. Run around the block. Dance to fast music. Play basketball with friends. Take your dog on a long walk.

Do Things You Enjoy

Do things you enjoy, like biking, swimming, playing sports, hanging out with friends, seeing a movie, or whatever else you like to do. Remember, it's okay to smile and have fun.

Make Your Own Book

You can write a story from memories you have of the person who is gone. Then draw illustrations to create your very own book.

Note to Parents

When a parent or loved one dies, a child's world, as he or she knew it, explodes. All of the things that a child assumed, counted on, and trusted in are no longer a certainty. Children, especially young children, are confused by such an abstract concept as death. It doesn't fit into their framework of concrete thinking.

More than anything, a grieving child needs to re-establish a sense of safety and security in the world. There are several things that parents can do to help their children process grief in a healthy way so they can trust the world and the people in it once again.

The father in *Remembering Mama* provides a wonderful example of how parents can help their grieving children. These are some of the techniques he uses that you may find useful as well.

Be present. To help children regain safety, let them know you will be available for them. Be there when they need to talk, cry, or be held.

Find support. It's very difficult to deal with your own grief and that of your children all by yourself. Find others who will be supportive over the many months of healing. In *Remembering Mama,* Grandma offers such support, helping to envelop the child in an emotional blanket of security.

Maintain connections. A large part of healthy grieving involves the ability to maintain connections with the person who died. This is the major theme of this book, and it illustrates the power of memory. Tell stories, sing favorite songs, visit familiar sites, and bring out the family photographs. Actively remembering the past can provide comfort in the present.

Nourish faith. Help your child, as Dad does, to believe that the body may die, but the spirit lives on. Believing that a loved one's soul continues to live can help children realize that they are not alone and that they continue to be loved.

Guiding a child through grief is a long-term, difficult process. But you will make it. Be present to your child. Answer questions. Hug. Cry. Hope. Believe. And remember. Always remember.

James P. Emswiler, M.A., M.Ed.
Co-founder of The Cove Center for Grieving Children and Their Families and author of *Guiding Your Child through Grief.*